PHONEME TRACK WORKBOOK

Laura Cryer

Published in association with David Fulton Publishers

SEMERC, Granada Television, Quay Street, Manchester M60 9EA

www.granada-learning.com

First published in Great Britain in 2004 by SEMERC, in association with David Fulton Publishers

10 9 8 7 6 5 4 3 2 1

SEMERC is a division of Granada Learning Limited, part of ITV plc.

British Library Cataloguing in Publication Data
A catalogue record for this book is available from the British Library.

ISBN 1-84312-138-7

Designed and typeset by Kenneth Burnley, Wirral, Cheshire
Printed and bound in Great Britain

PHONEME TRACK
WORKBOOK

By the same author:

Spell Track Workbook (Semerc) ISBN 1-84312-000-3
Word Track Workbook (Semerc) ISBN 1-84312-137-9

Contents

Introduction

The panic and frustration felt by struggling readers when not able to 'break the code' in reading is seen all too often. Children first learn to read following some consistent and dependable rules. They may be able to read 'mad bad lad sat on sad dad's lap' quite easily, but they then start to realise that vowel sounds become more uncertain – a vowel surrounded by consonants can become short, long or change out of all recognition (e.g. 'saw', 'new', 'work', 'car', 'fork'). Then they have to be able to correctly read similar looking but confusing words such as 'great', 'easy', 'bread', 'beard', 'bear', 'heard' as well as 'funny money'!

Spelling 'rules' are so complex that most children find learning to read and spell by only applying rigid decoding and encoding strategies ('sounding out' and 'breaking down') frustrating and stressful.

When coming across an unknown word, we have to help children to call upon *all* their key skills of reading: phonic (sound), graphic and word recognition (sight), syntax (grammatical knowledge), and semantic (contextual understanding) in harmony. It is a process that should become intuitive, easy and rapid, but is, unfortunately, often a painful and laborious one.

Word recognition skills alone are not enough to enable us to process all new words we meet in reading. Lack of phonemic knowledge causes many of the problems encountered by pupils who experience difficulty in reading at Key Stage 2.

Mary Williams (1998) points out that our teaching could reflect the 'Searchlights' model of the National Literacy Strategy, which suggests that teaching should be focused on one or more of the key skills. Each strategy is seen as interdependent, each contributing to overall understanding at text level gained through the ability to read words in sentences (Figure 1).

The English alphabet lacks a one-to-one correspondence between each sound in the language and the symbol that represents it. There are 44 phonemes in English, represented by 26 letters – this is the basis of our alphabetic code. A phoneme means a 'unit of sound' – this is the smallest or finest sound in speech that people can hear.

Individual phonemes become embedded in the flow of speech and are hard to hear and to disconnect. Our auditory system hears them as sets of overlapping sounds in syllable chunks. This means that as children master speaking fluently and effortlessly, their ability to hear individual phonemes within words can decline. We become unaware of phonemic

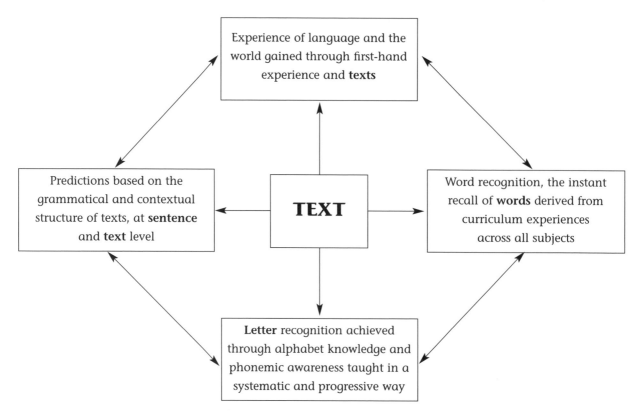

Figure 1: Combined model of the reading process (Williams 1998)

levels of speech because it is inefficient to be aware of it. Children must be taught to hear and be aware of individual phonemes in speech because they do not necessarily know that they are there. Many children cannot *hear* the units of sound the letters stand for. Without specific phonemic awareness training, phonics can make little sense and the spellings of words can only be learned by rote and reading is not able to be automatic. *Phoneme Track* aims to reinforce awareness of individual phonemes.

Research indicates that all young readers benefit from explicit assistance with phonemic awareness. Support for phonological awareness should occur in the early years and at Key Stage 1 to include the developmental stages of:

- awareness of syllables
- awareness of rhyme
- awareness of onset and rime
- sound isolation (identifying beginnings, middles and ends in words)
- phoneme manipulation – blending
- phoneme manipulation – substitution
- phoneme manipulation – deletion
- phoneme manipulation – reversal
- phoneme manipulation – transposition.

The consensus of recent research suggests that dyslexics have an early impairment in phonological skills that prevent them acquiring the auditory decoding skills necessary for reading and spelling, and that 'awareness that spoken language is composed of phonemes is an extremely important predictor of success in learning to read' (Adams 1990). These children require specific teaching that concentrates on phonological awareness.

We need to teach *all* children to understand that the letters on the page stand for specific sounds in their own speech, and then the matching of letters to sounds will make more sense.

However, consonants are very hard to 'unglue' from vowels. Many consonants in English are hard to *say* separately from a vowel sound. (Try saying /b/ by itself without saying /buh/). It is even more difficult to split sounds apart into phonemes when they are embedded in a word (can you hear and identify the five phonemes in /strong/, /dwells/, /crunch/?).

Most children can hear isolated phonemes (/f/, /l/, /m/) and make comparisons between them ('Is /d/ the same as /g/?'). The problems begin when phonemes are embedded within words.

The National Literacy Strategy recognises the importance of phonemic awareness training and focuses on hearing, identifying, segmenting and blending of phonemes. *Phoneme Track* aims to encourage learners to hear and see a change made to the phoneme sequence in words and helps to identify where in that sequence the change took place. The skills of phoneme manipulation are the ones that many children find particularly hard to master.

Changes can occur by:

- addition – a new phoneme comes in (/it/ becomes /sit/)

- deletion – a phoneme is taken away (/pat/ becomes /at/)

- substitution – one phoneme is replaced by another (/cap/ becomes /cup/).

Phoneme Track encourages learners to build up skill levels of phonemic awareness so that they can increase their confidence in coping with reading and spelling more complex words. *Phoneme Track* aims to be fun and motivational while supporting the improvement of phonemic awareness. The activities offer word-level work in an interesting and problem-solving way.

We need to encourage lots of talking, listening and playing with sounds and to promote a love of language. Teaching phonic rules is part of the process of learning to read and is a useful strategy in acquiring the skills of reading and writing. But we must not ignore the importance of praise and encouragement, encouraging risk without fear of failure and promoting the enjoyment and fun of language. *Phoneme Track* supports teachers in the inclusive classroom in their teaching of vital literacy skills.

This book will show children how to delete phonemes at the beginning, middle and end of words. Students can practise doing this on words with three phonemes, i.e. 'hit', 'cup', 'hair'; four phonemes, i.e. 'clap', 'frog' and 'place'; and five phonemes, i.e. 'struck', 'stream' and 'stand'. The student then works on the graphemes that represent those phonemes.

Laura Cryer
Special Educational Needs Publisher
Semerc/Granada Learning

Instructions

It is important that the learner understand the concepts of 'missing from', 'take away', 'without', 'left' in relation to the phonemes (sounds) in words. If necessary, link with practical activities, visual and auditory examples. For example, draw a picture of a car without a wheel – ask the question, 'What is missing?' – 'This is a car without a wheel.'

Talk about saying the word 'cat' without the phoneme /c/ to get the word 'at'.

A learner should understand that the sounds in a word can be broken up. The phoneme is each spoken sound and the grapheme is the written representation of that sound.

Each word is presented in a phoneme frame that puts each phoneme (individual sound) in separate boxes. The learner should look, read and say the word and take away the phoneme from either the beginning, end or middle of the word. Say the new word. A space is provided for the learner to write the new word. This could be on its own, in a sentence, with or without a picture, and so on, as directed by the teacher or carer with regard to specific learning objectives. The space has been deliberately left so that the individual is able to develop those activities that enable his/her most effective learning style.

The goal of these activities is the mastery of the concept of phoneme deletion thus developing phonological skills while working towards fluent word reading and improved spellings.

BEGINNINGS

Name _____ Date _____

- Read and say the word aloud.
- Now say the word without the phoneme at the **beginning** of the word.
- Write down the word you have made.

| s | our | |

| y | ear | |

| h | air | |

| p | air | |

I can read and write all the words in the phoneme frames   ☺   ☺   ☹

Name _____ Date _____

- Read and say the word aloud.
- Now say the word without the phoneme at the **beginning** of the word.
- Write down the word you have made.

h	i	s	

h	i	t	

f	a	n	

s	i	t	

I can read and write all the words in the phoneme frames ☺   ☺   ☹

Name _____ Date _____

- Read and say the word aloud.
- Now say the word without the phoneme at the **beginning** of the word.
- Write down the word you have made.

| c | a | t | |

| f | a | t | |

| h | a | t | |

| c | a | n | |

I can read and write all the words in the phoneme frames   ☹

Name _____ Date _____

- Read and say the word aloud.
- Now say the word without the phoneme at the **beginning** of the word.
- Write down the word you have made.

| c | o | n | |

| b | o | x | |

| c | u | p | |

| b | u | s | |

I can read and write all the words in the phoneme frames ☺   ☺   ☹

5

Name _____ Date _____

- Read and say the word aloud.
- Now say the word without the phoneme at the **beginning** of the word.
- Write down the word you have made.

b	a	ll	

b	i	ll	

f	o	x	

l	oa	f	

I can read and write all the words in the phoneme frames   ☺   ☺   ☹

6

Name _____ Date _____

- Read and say the word aloud.
- Now say the word without the phoneme at the **beginning** of the word.
- Write down the word you have made.

| b | oa | t | |

| r | a | ce | |

| m | i | ce | |

| d | a | te | |

I can read and write all the words in the phoneme frames ☺ ☺ ☹

7

Name _____ Date _____

- Read and say the word aloud.
- Now say the word without the phoneme at the **beginning** of the word.
- Write down the word you have made.

p	a	ge	

s	t	ar	

m	ar	k	

f	ar	m	

I can read and write all the words in the phoneme frames   ☺

Name _____ Date _____

- Read and say the word aloud.
- Now say the word without the phoneme at the **beginning** of the word.
- Write down the word you have made.

s	oa	k	

c	ar	t	

v	i	ce	

f	ow	l	

I can read and write all the words in the phoneme frames   ☺   ☺   ☹

9

Name _____ Date _____

- Read and say the word aloud.
- Now say the word without the phoneme at the **beginning** of the word.
- Write down the word you have made.

| d | ar | k | |

| p | l | ay | |

| b | l | ow | |

| l | ear | n | |

I can read and write all the words in the phoneme frames

Name _____ Date _____

- Read and say the word aloud.
- Now say the word without the phoneme at the **beginning** of the word.
- Write down the word you have made.

| wh | ee | l | |

| th | a | t | |

| th | r | ow | |

| ch | ar | m | |

I can read and write all the words in the phoneme frames ☺ ☺ ☹

11

Name _____ Date _____

- Read and say the word aloud.
- Now say the word without the phoneme at the **beginning** of the word.
- Write down the word you have made.

ch	ea	t	

s	c	ore	

p	r	ay	

I can read and write all the words in the phoneme frames   ☺   ☺   ☹

12

Name _____   Date _____

- Read and say the word aloud.
- Now say the word without the phoneme at the **beginning** of the word.
- Write down the word you have made.

| s | i | n | k | | | |

| s | a | n | d | | | |

| h | o | l | d | | | |

| s | e | l | f | | | |

I can read and write all the words in the phoneme frames   ☺   😐   ☹

Name _____ Date _____

- Read and say the word aloud.
- Now say the word without the phoneme at the **beginning** of the word.
- Write down the word you have made.

g	l	a	d	

c	l	a	p	

s	t	o	p	

s	p	o	t	

I can read and write all the words in the phoneme frames ☺ ☺ ☹

14

Name _____ Date _____

- Read and say the word aloud.
- Now say the word without the phoneme at the **beginning** of the word.
- Write down the word you have made.

| s | t | oo | l | |

| b | l | o | ck | |

| c | l | o | ck | |

| p | l | a | te | |

I can read and write all the words in the phoneme frames ☺

15

Name _____ Date _____

- Read and say the word aloud.
- Now say the word without the phoneme at the **beginning** of the word.
- Write down the word you have made.

| p | l | a | ce | |

| g | o | l | d | |

| t | w | i | n | |

| t | r | a | p | |

I can read and write all the words in the phoneme frames

16

Name _____ Date _____

- Read and say the word aloud.
- Now say the word without the phoneme at the **beginning** of the word.
- Write down the word you have made.

| t | r | i | p | |

| b | r | a | ve | |

| p | l | a | ne | |

| p | r | i | ce | |

I can read and write all the words in the phoneme frames ☺

17

Name _____ Date _____

- Read and say the word aloud.
- Now say the word without the phoneme at the **beginning** of the word.
- Write down the word you have made.

| g | r | u | b | |

| t | r | ai | n | |

| d | r | a | t | |

| s | m | i | le | |

I can read and write all the words in the phoneme frames   ☺   ☺   ☹

18

Name _____ Date _____

- Read and say the word aloud.
- Now say the word without the phoneme at the **beginning** of the word.
- Write down the word you have made.

| r | i | n | k | |

| b | r | ai | n | |

| f | r | o | ck | |

| s | p | e | ck | |

I can read and write all the words in the phoneme frames   ☺

19

Name _____ Date _____

- Read and say the word aloud.
- Now say the word without the phoneme at the **beginning** of the word.
- Write down the word you have made.

| s | n | ai | l | |

| s | t | o | p | |

| g | l | o | ve | |

| c | l | i | p | |

I can read and write all the words in the phoneme frames ☺

20

Name _____ Date _____

- Read and say the word aloud.
- Now say the word without the phoneme at the **beginning** of the word.
- Write down the word you have made.

| s | l | igh | t | |

| f | r | igh | t | |

| s | qu | a | d | |

| s | w | i | sh | |

I can read and write all the words in the phoneme frames ☺ ☺ ☹

21

Name _____ Date _____

- Read and say the word aloud.
- Now say the word without the phoneme at the **beginning** of the word.
- Write down the word you have made.

| b | r | igh | t | |

| f | l | u | te | |

| b | r | i | de | |

I can read and write all the words in the phoneme frames ☺ ☺ ☹

22

Name _____ Date _____

- Read and say the word aloud.
- Now say the word without the phoneme at the **beginning** of the word.
- Write down the word you have made.

p	l	u	m	p	

c	r	e	s	t	

b	r	i	s	k	

s	t	r	i	p	

I can read and write all the words in the phoneme frames ☺ ☺ ☹

23

ENDINGS

Name _____ Date _____

- Read and say the word aloud.
- Now say the word without the phoneme at the **end** of the word.
- Write down the word you have made.

| h | er | b | |

| b | ar | k | |

| p | aw | n | |

| f | or | k | |

I can read and write all the words in the phoneme frames

Name _____ Date _____

- Read and say the word aloud.
- Now say the word without the phoneme at the **end** of the word.
- Write down the word you have made.

| f | ir | m | |

| b | ee | p | |

| t | oo | l | |

| l | aw | n | |

I can read and write all the words in the phoneme frames ☺

27

Name _____ Date _____

- Read and say the word aloud.
- Now say the word without the phoneme at the **end** of the word.
- Write down the word you have made.

| c | ar | t | |

| t | ea | ch | |

| n | ew | t | |

I can read and write all the words in the phoneme frames   ☺   ☺   ☹

Name _____ Date _____

· Read and say the word aloud.

· Now say the word without the phoneme at the **end** of the word.

· Write down the word you have made.

| m | e | n | d | |

| b | a | n | d | |

| d | e | n | t | |

| b | ur | n | t | |

I can read and write all the words in the phoneme frames   ☺   😐   ☹

29

Name _____ Date _____

- Read and say the word aloud.
- Now say the word without the phoneme at the **end** of the word.
- Write down the word you have made.

| p | i | n | k | |

| f | l | ow | n | |

| ch | i | p | s | |

| s | u | n | k | |

I can read and write all the words in the phoneme frames ☺   😐

Name _____ Date _____

- Read and say the word aloud.
- Now say the word without the phoneme at the **end** of the word.
- Write down the word you have made.

| w | i | n | k | |

| w | i | n | d | |

| t | e | n | d | |

| p | ai | n | t | |

I can read and write all the words in the phoneme frames ☺

31

Name _____ Date _____

- Read and say the word aloud.
- Now say the word without the phoneme at the **end** of the word.
- Write down the word you have made.

| b | u | n | ch | |

| w | i | n | ch | |

| f | or | t | y | |

| h | u | m | p | |

I can read and write all the words in the phoneme frames   ☺   😐   ☹

Name _____ Date _____

- Read and say the word aloud.
- Now say the word without the phoneme at the **end** of the word.
- Write down the word you have made.

b	u	s	k

b	a	n	k

s	i	n	k

w	a	s	p

I can read and write all the words in the phoneme frames ☺ 😐 ☹

33

Name _____ Date _____

- Read and say the word aloud.
- Now say the word without the phoneme at the **end** of the word.
- Write down the word you have made.

d	r	aw	n	

I can read and write all the words in the phoneme frames ☺ ☺ ☹

Name _____ Date _____

- Read and say the word aloud.
- Now say the word without the phoneme at the **end** of the word.
- Write down the word you have made.

| b | r | a | n | d | |

| p | l | a | n | t | |

| p | l | u | m | p | |

I can read and write all the words in the phoneme frames ☺ ☺ ☹

35

MIDDLES

Name _____ Date _____

- Read and say the word aloud.
- Now say the word without the phoneme in the **middle** (shaded part) of the word.
- Write down the word you have made.

c	l	ue	

f	r	ee	

d	r	ew	

s	c	ore	

I can read and write all the words in the phoneme frames   ☺   ☺   ☹

Name _____ Date _____

- Read and say the word aloud.
- Now say the word without the phoneme in the **middle** (shaded part) of the word.
- Write down the word you have made.

t r ee

s w ay

p r ay

I can read and write all the words in the phoneme frames ☺

39

Name _____ Date _____

- Read and say the word aloud.
- Now say the word without the phoneme in the **middle** (shaded part) of the word.
- Write down the word you have made.

| c | l | a | p | |

| f | r | o | g | |

| t | r | a | p | |

| f | i | s | t | |

I can read and write all the words in the phoneme frames ☺   😐   ☹

40

Name _____ Date _____

- Read and say the word aloud.
- Now say the word without the phoneme in the **middle** (shaded part) of the word.
- Write down the word you have made.

s k i p

s l i p

s p i n

s p i t

I can read and write all the words in the phoneme frames ☺

Name _____ Date _____

- Read and say the word aloud.
- Now say the word without the phoneme in the **middle** (shaded part) of the word.
- Write down the word you have made.

| s | a | l | t | |

| s | p | oo | n | |

| b | e | s | t | |

| p | l | a | n | |

I can read and write all the words in the phoneme frames ☺ ☺ ☹

42

Name _____ Date _____

- Read and say the word aloud.
- Now say the word without the phoneme in the **middle** (shaded part) of the word.
- Write down the word you have made.

| s | m | e | ll | |

| s | m | o | ck | |

| s | m | a | ck | |

| r | oo | s | t | |

I can read and write all the words in the phoneme frames ☺

43

Name _____   Date _____

- Read and say the word aloud.
- Now say the word without the phoneme in the **middle** (shaded part) of the word.
- Write down the word you have made.

| b | l | a | ck | |

| b | r | u | sh | |

| d | r | i | p | |

| l | o | s | t | |

I can read and write all the words in the phoneme frames   ☺

44

Name _____ Date _____

- Read and say the word aloud.
- Now say the word without the phoneme in the **middle** (shaded part) of the word.
- Write down the word you have made.

| t | r | a | p | |

| b | e | l | t | |

| b | a | n | d | |

| h | a | n | d | |

I can read and write all the words in the phoneme frames ☺

Name _____ Date _____

- Read and say the word aloud.
- Now say the word without the phoneme in the **middle** (shaded part) of the word.
- Write down the word you have made.

| s | n | a | p | |

| s | p | i | ll | |

| s | l | i | t | |

| s | t | r | ay | |

I can read and write all the words in the phoneme frames ☺   ☺   ☹

46

Name _____ Date _____

- Read and say the word aloud.
- Now say the word without the phoneme in the **middle** (shaded part) of the word.
- Write down the word you have made.

| s | t | i | ck | | |

| s | t | a | le | | |

| t | r | ie | d | | |

| b | r | a | t | | |

I can read and write all the words in the phoneme frames

47

Name _____   Date _____

- Read and say the word aloud.
- Now say the word without the phoneme in the **middle** (shaded part) of the word.
- Write down the word you have made.

| l | e | f | t | |

| l | i | f | t | |

| g | a | p | s | |

| l | a | m | p | |

I can read and write all the words in the phoneme frames   ☺   ☺

48

Name _____ Date _____

- Read and say the word aloud.
- Now say the word without the phoneme in the **middle** (shaded part) of the word.
- Write down the word you have made.

| s | e | n | t | |

| b | e | n | t | |

| b | e | n | d | |

| m | e | l | t | |

I can read and write all the words in the phoneme frames

Name _____ Date _____

- Read and say the word aloud.
- Now say the word without the phoneme in the **middle** (shaded part) of the word.
- Write down the word you have made.

n	e	x	t	

w	e	l	d	

b	l	ea	t	

g	r	a	te	

I can read and write all the words in the phoneme frames   ☹

Name _____ Date _____

- Read and say the word aloud.
- Now say the word without the phoneme in the **middle** (shaded part) of the word.
- Write down the word you have made.

| w | e | s | t | |

| w | e | n | t | |

| v | e | n | t | |

| d | r | aw | n | |

I can read and write all the words in the phoneme frames ☺

Name _____ Date _____

- Read and say the word aloud.
- Now say the word without the phoneme in the **middle** (shaded part) of the word.
- Write down the word you have made.

| l | i | s | p | |

| c | oa | s | t | |

| p | u | m | p | |

| s | l | u | m | |

I can read and write all the words in the phoneme frames ☺ ☺ ☹

52

Name _____ Date _____

- Read and say the word aloud.
- Now say the word without the phoneme in the **middle** (shaded part) of the word.
- Write down the word you have made.

| b | l | u | sh | |

| p | l | a | ne | |

| qu | i | l | t | |

| f | a | c | t | |

I can read and write all the words in the phoneme frames

53

Name _____   Date _____

- Read and say the word aloud.
- Now say the word without the phoneme in the **middle** (shaded part) of the word.
- Write down the word you have made.

b l ea t

s p oi l

f l igh t

sh u n t

I can read and write all the words in the phoneme frames   ☺   😐   ☹

54

Name _____ Date _____

- Read and say the word aloud.
- Now say the word without the phoneme in the **middle** (shaded part) of the word.
- Write down the word you have made.

| p | o | m | p | |

| t | r | i | ck | |

| s | p | ee | d | |

| n | e | s | t | |

I can read and write all the words in the phoneme frames ☺ ☺ ☹

55

Name _____ Date _____

- Read and say the word aloud.
- Now say the word without the phoneme in the **middle** (shaded part) of the word.
- Write down the word you have made.

| d | r | i | ve | |

| s | n | a | ck | |

| t | r | i | p | |

| j | e | s | t | |

I can read and write all the words in the phoneme frames   ☺   ☺   ☹

56

Name _____ Date _____

- Read and say the word aloud.
- Now say the word without the phoneme in the **middle** (shaded part) of the word.
- Write down the word you have made.

b	oa	s	t	

p	u	m	p	

I can read and write all the words in the phoneme frames ☺   ☺   ☹

Name _____ Date _____

- Read and say the word aloud.
- Now say the word without the phoneme in the **middle** (shaded part) of the word.
- Write down the word you have made.

| s | t | r | u | ck | |

| s | t | r | ea | m | |

| s | t | a | n | d | |

| c | l | a | m | p | |

I can read and write all the words in the phoneme frames ☺

58

Name _____ Date _____

- Read and say the word aloud.
- Now say the word without the phoneme in the **middle** (shaded part) of the word.
- Write down the word you have made.

t r a m p

b l i n d

e x i s t

t w i s t

I can read and write all the words in the phoneme frames ☺

Name _____ Date _____

- Read and say the word aloud.
- Now say the word without the phoneme in the **middle** (shaded part) of the word.
- Write down the word you have made.

| g | r | a | s | p | |

| s | p | l | i | t | |

I can read and write all the words in the phoneme frames   ☺

60

Name _____ Date _____

I can read and write all the words in the phoneme frames   ☹

Name _____   Date _____

I can read and write all the words in the phoneme frames   ☺

Name _____ Date _____

I can read and write all the words in the phoneme frames ☺

Name _____ Date _____

I can read and write all the words in the phoneme frames

Useful Reading

Adams, M. (1990) *Beginning to Read.* London: Heinemann.

Bryant, P. and Bradley, L. (1985) *Children's Reading Problems.* Oxford: Blackwell.

Burnett, A. and Wylie, J. (2002) *SoundAround.* London: David Fulton Publishers.

DfEE (1998) *The National Literacy Strategy: Framework for Teaching.* London: DfEE.

Frith, U. (1985) *Beneath the Surface of Development Dyslexia.* In J. Marshall, K. Patterson and M. Coltheart (eds) *Surface Dyslexia in Adults and Children.* London: Routledge and Kegan Paul.

Goswami, U. and Bryant, P. (1990) *Phonological Skills and Learning to Read.* London: Psychology Press.

Hatcher, P. (1994) *Sound Linkage: An Integrated Programme for Overcoming Reading Difficulties.* London: Whurr Publishers.

Layton, L. and Deeny, K. (2002) *Sound Practice: Phonological Awareness in the Classroom.* London: David Fulton Publishers.

McGuiness, D. (1998) *Why Children Can't Read and What We Can Do About It?* London: Penguin.

Ott, Philomena (1997) *How to Detect and Manage Dyslexia.* London: Heinemann.

Raymond, S. (2001) *Supporting Dyslexic Pupils 7–14 Across the Curriculum.* London: David Fulton Publishers.

Riddick, B., Wolfe, J. and Lumsdon, D. (2002) *Dyslexia: A Practical Guide for Teachers and Parents.* London: David Fulton Publishers.

Thomson, M. (ed.) (2003) *Dyslexia Included: A Whole School Approach.* London: David Fulton Publishers.

Tod, J. (2000) *Dyslexia.* London: David Fulton Publishers.

Walton, M. (1998) *Teaching Reading and Spelling to Dyslexic Children.* London: David Fulton Publishers.

Williams, M. (1998) *A Study which Explores the Impact of the English National Curriculum on the Work of Teachers at Key Stage 2,* PhD Thesis (unpublished), Brunel University.